Landing That Professional Job

Landing That Professional Job

A Career Guide for College Students

Diana Barnett

LLJORDAN PRESS
Landing That Professional Job: A Career Guide for College Students
Diana Barnett
Copyright © 2016 by Diana Barnett

Published in the United States by LLJORDAN Press
ISBN: 0997526203
ISBN 9780997526202
Library of Congress Control Number: 2016907050
LLJordan Press, Grand Junction, CO

Contents

Begin with the end in mind. As Stephen Covey suggests in *7 Habits of Highly Effective People*, you need to visualize your goal. Whatever you have in mind for your future, be specific, and keep your eye on that goal so it constantly serves as your guiding star. Kind of like the old saying, "If you don't know where you're headed, you'll probably end up somewhere else." You want to *know* where you are going!

Explore Careers

Each journey has a beginning, and the earlier yours can start, the better. Middle school and high school is the time to begin thinking about careers. Many secondary schools offer interest, personality, and ability-based inventories that will provide an introduction to various occupational themes. Utilize this information and research the jobs suggested in your assessment reports. High school counselors are trained in career education.

- Make an appointment with a counselor at your school early to begin talking about careers in which you have an interest.
- Shadow some professionals in careers in which you have an interest. You can find out if you like the work environment, the work itself, and what it would take to get yourself there.
- Take advantage of any classes or activities that offer career exploration opportunities.
- Visit with people you know who have similar careers.

CHOOSE A MAJOR – THE RIGHT MAJOR

What are you majoring in? Everyone asks you this question. The question they probably should be asking is, "What job are you planning on when you graduate?" A major is an in-depth study of a discipline—it is not the work you will be doing after you complete your degree. That's why it is important to look at careers that are a good match for you *before* choosing that major.

Many majors leave no doubt as to the career destination. Education, nursing, and engineering are all good examples. Business, biology or communications, on the other hand, offer coursework in a smattering of areas and can point to any number of jobs. So it is important to research particular jobs before you decide on the major. How?

People need different sets of skills to be happy and successful in a career. They need, obviously, to have the appropriate education and training, but they also need a particular set of social skills and personality traits to complete the picture. For example, someone who loves being outdoors because of recreational hobbies decides to major in biology. They finish their degree and find employment with the U.S. Forest Service tramping around solo gathering data on plants and wildlife in the area. As much as they love the outdoors, the routine becomes a little boring after a while. And because this individual is very social, the opportunity to work with others on a regular basis is just not part of this particular job.

So researching careers—specific jobs—is important. Begin with the end in mind. Now is the time to get serious about narrowing down that career.

- Know thyself! Take an interest and personality inventory that will help you learn more about yourself and what occupations you would be suited for and enjoy. Visit your local job service office or your college career center to see what is available.
- Have a professional career specialist interpret the results of the assessment for you. These are research-based tools and require a trained individual to help you gain the best understanding of the information.
- Research the careers that appear on your assessment results. Use *Occupational Outlook Handbook* (http://www.bls.gov/ooh/) and *O*Net Online* (http://www.onetonline.org/) to learn about work environment, job growth projections, degree and background needed, and the nature of the work.
- Once you narrow your choices down to a few careers, connect with professionals who do those jobs to confirm if these would be a good fit for you. Does the nature of the work fit your strengths, abilities and personality? Is there a demand for these jobs? What is the level of education or training needed for entry level into the jobs?
- Knowing what degree is required by these jobs, research colleges that offer these degrees. Look at the coursework you would have to take, entrance requirements of the schools, affordability, and job placement levels at graduation.
- The bottom line is, you need to first choose a career that is compatible with your abilities, interests and personality. Now, what major is going to get you there?

THE BIG IDEA!

Gather information about yourself and research jobs that you find interesting. Shadow individuals in these professions to gain a better understanding of the work environment and skills needed! Use resources available to you—your high school counselors and college career professionals. You need to know as much about yourself as possible in order to make the best match between you and your future career.

Do Your *Best* Work as a Student

Once you begin your college classes, being the most successful student you can be is now your *job*.

- Attend classes regularly.
- Study hard.
- Do your homework.
- Understand the material.
- Ask questions.
- Collaborate with others.
- Be ethical.
- Organize your life and your information.
- Develop a network.

All of the above are important as your school habits become your work habits, and you want good ones.

WHAT DO EMPLOYERS WANT?

Feedback from employers shows they seek employees who are dependable and punctual. They work hard to learn their job and if they have questions, they ask. They organize their work and prioritize the tasks at hand. Employees are team players when the job calls for this, but they should also be independent workers. They develop strong professional relationships with colleagues and supervisors and add them to their network. They do the right thing for the right reason and are honest.

WORK IN AN INTERNSHIP

Another important thing employers are looking for is work experience in your field. One way to meet this criteria is to do an internship for a summer or a semester that allows you to apply your learning in a real job. Internships are required for many major areas of study, but not all. Some programs do not require one, but students should participate in one. Internships are critical to gaining professional employment when you finish your program. Seek assistance in finding one from your faculty advisor and from your college career services office. Many employers post internship opportunities on websites for job postings.

Another way to get related experience is to get a summer job or volunteer for a position in your field. While you may not yet have the academic requirements for specific professional jobs, you can gain experience in the environment in which you may be working later on.

Apply for a Professional Job

It's still several months until graduation, but you don't want to wait until the last minute to begin preparing and applying for that first professional job. Start by creating the document that illustrates what you have to offer a company—your resume.

GETTING YOUR PAPERWORK IN ORDER

RESUME VS. CURRICULUM VITAE

The majority of professional jobs requires a resume that is concise and to the point in displaying the important skills and background you have to bring to a position. A curriculum vitae is generally used for jobs primarily in an academic setting. Because a resume format is more widely required and used, we'll begin with writing a resume.

Create Your Resume

Your resume will be the first introduction a potential employer has to you, so make it a good one.

IMPORTANT STRATEGIES FOR AN EFFECTIVE RESUME:

- Choose a standard, readable font
- Use bold-facing, underlining and bullets
- Use a logical, well organized layout
- Make it concise and one page if possible
- Make it relevant to the job, with the related information close to the top

GETTING STARTED – KNOW THE JOB!

You are preparing your resume based on a particular job for which you want to apply. You'll want to show how qualified you are for this job in your resume. Print off the job description. Take a highlighter and mark all of the requirements for this position—both task-related and personal qualities. Use this as a guideline as you create your resume, including skills and experience that you have that meet the requirements. Even if you don't have a job you're interested in at the moment, find one that would be an ideal choice, and use it as a guideline.

If you have a particular job for which you are applying, **be completely knowledgeable** about the job duties and requirements. **Print** out the job description. **Highlight** main duties and all skills, education and experience required.

Family YMCA offers a variety of youth development and youth sports programs on a year round basis. The Sports & Recreation Coordinator will plan and implement the diverse range of youth & adult sports-focused programming for our YMCA.

Qualifications

- Candidate must be a master of time management & communication, and be a team player with exceptional organizational and marketing skills to handle managing multiple programs simultaneously.
- HS Diploma required, 2 or 4 year degree is a plus.
- Candidate should possess a strong understanding of the YMCA mission and core values (to be taught in all programs) and a strong desire to develop and deliver high quality programs.

Essential Functions

- The Sports & Recreation Coordinator should be a self-starter, able to work independently, be well organized, positive, enthusiastic, caring individual who enjoys working with youth and families. The candidate should have a high ability to recruit, retain, and coach staff/volunteers; while working within a team atmosphere, exemplifies a proactive, hands-on, and professional appearance and work ethic.
- Lead the recruiting and training of 50 volunteers with a goal of 800 participants for youth sports programs and leagues. Maintain relationships with city parks and recreation departments, parents, vendors, schools, community partners, and other local agencies. Assist with marketing the programs in order to increase awareness and participation. Maintain relations with the community and its representatives, interpreting the YMCA and its work.
- Promotes youth involvement through programs, engages & connects community youth for long term retention. Set up multiple facilities (both on and off-site) for games, practices, special events, etc.
- Provide overall administration for the youth & adult sports & recreation programing. Responsible for developing, marketing, implementing and expanding current programs. Assist with annual fundraising Campaign. Implement all YMCA policies and procedures for risk management / safety for all staff, volunteers and participants.
- Develop, manage and oversee an $85,000 budget determined by program growth and retention through well executed, quality fee-based programs.
- Supervise part time and seasonal staff as well as over 30 volunteers
- Responsible for developing, planning, organizing, promoting, preparing, running, monitoring, implementing, scheduling and evaluating all youth @ adult sports programming including, but not limited Jr. Lakers, Futsal, Adult Basketball; and will work with the other department heads to promote their programs as well.

Refer to the information you have highlighted as you are creating your resume. The best places to customize your work are in your skills section and the duties you list under your work experience. You'll want to make your resume reflect the required skills and background as closely and honestly as you can.

WHAT TO INCLUDE?

A resume is a concise, organized picture of you, and should include these basic section headings:

- Heading
- Objective
- Education

- Work Experience
- Skills and Strengths
- Honors and Awards
- Campus and/or Community Involvement

Although you'll want to customize your resume for a particular job, there are some standard sections you'll need to include. And there may be some additional sections that you'll want to add to fit your background and experience. Those are included in the following examples as *optional headings*.

SECTION 1: THE HEADING

Steven Parkman
3055 Smith Road, Littleton, CO, 80126
303-335-5424 sparkm@gmail.com
www.linkedin.com/stevenparkman

You'll need to include **your full name, mailing address, phone number, e-mail address, and LinkedIn URL**. This important information will appear at the top of your resume and lets an employer know how you may be reached for an interview. Make sure you use your legal name as it appears on your transcripts or other important documents. Because you must often include a copy of your transcripts as part of your application packet, you will want to use the same name so there is no confusion. If you have another name—a nickname or middle name—which you prefer to be called, you can put that in parentheses between your first and last name.

Make sure the e-mail address that you use has a professional look. You've outgrown the cute one you used in middle school. Don't jeopardize the otherwise professional appearance of your resume by including an inappropriate address.

For example:

Henry (Jack) Blackburn
hjblackburn@gmail.com

SECTION 2: THE OBJECTIVE
To obtain the position of Sports Manager with Denver Sports where I can use my leadership skills and my passion to promote lifelong fitness and recreation.

This could also be called the goal or purpose of your resume, and will be the first section under your heading. You'll want to be specific for a particular job. The objective statement should be followed by a period—even though it is not a complete sentence. The objective statement is optional, but it is one way a resume can be customized for a particular job. After your contact information, it is the first item a potential employer sees. He may appreciate the fact that the job title and company are included in your resume. If the company has several openings, it also alerts an employer to the position for which you are applying.

SECTION 3: EDUCATION

Colorado Mesa University (CMU), Grand Junction, CO
Bachelor of Science, May 2016
Major: Sport Management
GPA: 3.6/4.0

Include the institution name, location, graduation date, degree, major, and GPA (optional and only if above 3.0). If you have a degree from another institution, list the most recent or current work first. You only need to include another school if you received a degree there. High school information is not used on a college resume.

SECTION 4: INTERNSHIP

Grand Junction Rockies, Grand Junction, CO Summers, 2015 - 2016
Intern

- Participated in weekly management meetings to evaluate work and schedule projects
- Assisted and trained summer employees in the setup and operations of the concession/gift shop area
- Planned and implemented a VIP Night to recognize local team sponsors
- Researched marketing ideas and promoted sales by creating and implementing an email blast as a marketing tool

Because most students do not have much major-related work experience, it is important to include pertinent information next to your education section that supports your preparation for a professional position. If you have completed an internship, include this information next under its own heading. Employers want to hire competent people who bring the most relevant background with them.

If you do not have an internship to list, and have a little additional space, you may want to include a list of coursework you have taken. Bulleted lists are a handy way to display these, also lending a little variety to the layout of your resume. If you choose to include a section with your coursework, select classes that are most relevant to the particular job for which you are applying.

If you have additional training and/or certificates, create a separate section heading and list those, the certifying agency and dates, as in the example below.

SECTION 5: HIGHLIGHTED COURSEWORK

Leadership & Ethics in Sports	Sport Law & Risk Management
Sport Operations	Economics & Finance in Sport Management
Sales & Sales Management	Sport Management

OPTIONAL SECTION: ADDITIONAL TRAINING/CERTIFICATIONS

- NREMT- Basic, State of Colorado, 2015
- CPR/AED, State of Colorado, Denver, 2015

If you have completed research or assisted a faculty member with his, certainly include this under a section titled, Academic Research. This would be located right after your Education section.

OPTIONAL SECTION: ACADEMIC RESEARCH

Benson, Adam and Dr. Howard Smith. Effects of wildland fire on *Juniperus sibirica* in the Pacific Northwest. Washington State University, 2015 – 2016.

If you have worked on a special project for a class that allowed you to use programs and skills related to requirements for a job for which you are applying, include this information in a section titled, Special Academic Projects.

OPTIONAL SECTION: SPECIAL ACADEMIC PROJECTS

Gonzales, Steven and others. External knee adduction moment analysis. Work to fulfill requirements for Mechanical Engineering Senior Project, University of Colorado, Boulder, August 2015 – Present.

- Designed a device to measure an individual's gait to correlate with the external knee adduction moment, with the objective being to choose the optimum variable stiffness shoe.

Including particular skills that you possess is another way of customizing your resume and showing that you are a good match for the job requirements.

SECTION 6: SKILLS AND STRENGTHS

Leadership	Organized/Detail Oriented	Supervisory
Problem Solving	Microsoft Office Proficient	Budgeting
Effective Communicator	Management	Staff Trainer

This section should be a combination of work-related skills and personal strengths--sometimes called soft skills. These may not all be apparent in the duty section of your work experience section, so it is important to point these out to potential employers. This section usually is located directly above your *Work Experience* section. Know that whatever you choose to include in this section—or any part of your resume-- is fair game in an interview. An employer may ask you to give an example of how you have used this skill or strength in a work situation.

Then, of course, if you do happen to have some work experience that is directly related to your field of study, include that in a section called *Related Work Experience*.

OPTIONAL SECTION: RELATED WORK EXPERIENCE

Soccer Camps Incorporated, Boulder, Colorado   Summer, 2014
Coach

- Recruited and trained 12 – 14 year-olds for traveling soccer team
- Collaborated with parents to facilitate team fundraising efforts
- Created summer match schedules and organized team travel
- Maintained current and accurate budget for team operations

If you do have a section titled, *Related Work Experience*, you can include other job experience you've had under the heading, *Additional Work Experience*. If you do not have work experience that is specifically related to your field of study, as in the example above, the next section in your resume will be *Work Experience.* All jobs listed will begin in reverse chronological order, with the most recent first.

SECTION 7: WORK EXPERIENCE

J.C. Penney, Littleton, Colorado   May, 2013 – September, 2015
Sales Associate

- Assisted customers with information and purchases
- Worked closely with colleagues and supervisors to provide a quality customer experience
- Trained new employees (3-4 monthly) in company policy, procedures and safety
- Represented the company in a positive and professional manner
- Promoted to Assistant Manager after three months because of increase in sales

Begin each job duty with a strong action verb. Use present tense if you are currently at that job, past tense if you no longer have the job. It is important to expand a duty description to tell as much about your responsibility as possible. How many customers did you serve on a shift? How many employees did you train? Did you receive a promotion because of your work? Under this heading, you can choose the number of jobs you include. If you are a nontraditional student, you only have to include ten years of work history. Or, if you have held several jobs, but want to include those most applicable to the job for which you are currently applying, you can use the heading *Selected Work Experience.* This implies to an employer that you have more work experience, but you are choosing to include that which he/she would find more applicable to the job for which you are applying.

SECTION 8: HONORS AND AWARDS

- Dean's List, Colorado Mesa University, Grand Junction, CO, 2014, 2015 (3 semesters)
- Recipient, Senior Scholarship, Kiwanis Club, Littleton, CO, 2013
- Outstanding Sales Associate, J.C. Penney, Littleton, CO, 2013

If you have something you can include here, do it. Receiving an award indicates achievement in a variety of areas. It can show initiative, leadership, creativity or academic success—all valuable qualities to bring to a professional job!

SECTION 9: CAMPUS AND COMMUNITY INVOLVEMENT

- Volunteer, Catholic Outreach Soup Kitchen, Boulder, Colorado 2013 – 2014
- Member, Men's Soccer, Colorado Mesa University, Grand Junction, Colorado 2013 – 2015
- Member, Sport Management Club, Colorado Mesa University, 2014 - 2016

Employers like to see that you have expanded your horizons and can show involvement outside your classes. Volunteer work always looks impressive on a resume. Create a section title that fits your experience. If you only have activities on campus, then your section should be *Campus Involvement.*

HOW TO CUSTOMIZE FOR A PARTICULAR JOB.

You'll want to prepare your resume to meet the requirements of the job for which you are applying as closely as possible.

How? Print a copy of the job description. Use a highlighter to mark the requirements of that job. Include information on your resume that matches these requirements as best you can. If you possess the skills and personal qualities that are required, you can list these in a bulleted skills list or include them under the duties in jobs you've held. Be honest. Only include skills and experience that you actually have. In your objective, specify the job title for which you are applying, and the company name. This shows a potential employer that you have created this resume for his position!

THE BIG IDEA!

Your resume needs to be a reflection of you and the skills and strengths that you bring to the job. Your personality should show through. It also should be customized for the particular job for which you are applying. Often, new graduates don't have work experience related to their major, so include everything that shows your preparation: specialized coursework, internships, research, academic projects, and organizations and volunteer activities. Use only section headings needed to show your unique experience. It is important that it is free of grammar and spelling errors and well written. Sometimes it helps to talk about your background and skills with someone to make sure you include all relevant information appropriate for the job. Seek the help of career services professionals on your campus to create the best resume possible.

Steven Parkman

sparkm@gmail.com
www.linkedin.com/stevenparkman

3055 Smith Road
Littleton, CO 80126
303-335-5424

Objective
To obtain the position of Sports Manager with Denver Sports where I can contribute my leadership skills and my passion to promote lifelong fitness and recreation.

Education
Colorado Mesa University, Grand Junction, CO
Bachelor of Science, May 2016
Major: Sport Management

Additional Training/Certifications
NREMT - Basic, State of Colorado, 2015
CPR/AED, State of Colorado, Denver, 2015

Internship
Intern, Grand Junction Rockies, Grand Junction, CO, Summer, 2015
- Participated in weekly management meetings to evaluate work and schedule projects
- Assisted and trained summer employees in the setup and operations of the concession/gift shop area
- Planned and implemented a VIP Night to recognize local team sponsors
- Researched marketing ideas and promoted sales by creating and implementing an email blast as a marketing tool

Highlighted Coursework
- Leadership & Ethics in Sports
- Sport Operations
- Sales & Sales Management
- Sport Law & Risk Management
- Economics & Finance in Sport Management
- Sport Management

Skills/Strengths
- Leadership
- Effective Communicator
- Staff Trainer
- Organized/Detail Oriented
- Microsoft Office Proficient
- Management
- Supervisory
- Budgeting
- Problem Solving

Related Work Experience
Coach, Soccer Camps Incorporated, Boulder, CO, Summer, 2014
- Recruited and trained 12 - 14 year-olds for traveling soccer team
- Collaborated with parents to facilitate team fundraising efforts
- Created summer match schedules and organized team travel
- Maintained current and accurate budget for team operations

Additional Work Experience
Sales Associate/Assistant Manager, J.C. Penney, Littleton, CO, May, 2013 - September, 2015
- Assisted customers with information and purchases
- Worked closely with colleagues and supervisors to provide a quality customer experience
- Trained new employees (3-4 monthly) in company policy, procedures and safety
- Promoted to Assistant Manager after three months because of increase in sales

Honors and Awards
- Dean's List, Colorado Mesa University, Grand Junction, CO, 2014, 2015 (3 Semesters)
- Recipient, Senior Scholarship, Kiwanis Club, Littleton, CO, 2014
- Outstanding Sales Associate, J.C. Penney, Littleton, CO, 2013

Campus and Community Involvement
- Volunteer, Catholic Outreach Soup Kitchen, Boulder, CO 2013 - 2014
- Member, Men's Soccer, Colorado Mesa University, Grand Junction, CO 2013 - Present
- Member, Sport Management Club, Colorado Mesa University, 2014 - Present

References

Y ou'll want to include the names and contact information for three solid references who can attest to your employability. Potential employers want to know what kind of worker you are, if you are dependable and show up on time. They also want to know about your attitude on the job and if you were able to work successfully with others. Obviously, you'll want to select individuals who will give you a positive recommendation. Individuals to ask include work supervisors, co-workers, coaches, and faculty members who can talk about your attitude, dedication, and work ethic. It is not appropriate to include friends or family members.

Once you have your list, contact each individual by phone or personal visit, and ask them if they will serve as a positive reference for you. Tell them about the jobs for which you are applying, and give them a copy of your resume. Ask them how they would prefer to be contacted and include only the information they have provided. Names of references are not included as part of your resume. They are listed on a separate document. Submit a list of references when asked by a potential employer as part of the application process. If the employer does not ask for your list in advance, present it to him/her during your interview.

The format of your reference sheet should look similar to the heading of your resume. Copy and paste your information header from your resume to the top of your resume document. Then center the word REFERENCES a few spaces from your header. Your references should be centered in the main body of your document. Include reference's full name, title, relationship to you, address, phone number and e-mail. List as much information as you have been given permission to provide.

Steven Parkman

sparkm@gmail.com
www.linkedin.com/stevenparkman

3055 Smith Road
Littleton, CO 80126
303-335-5424

References

Mr. Mark Smith
Athletic Director
Internship Adviser
Central High School
300 Monroe Ave.
Grand Junction, CO 81501
970-241-6678
msmith@chs.k12.co.us

Janean Hadley
Assistant Manager
Former Supervisor
Fairview Recreation Center
1593 White Street
Littleton, CO 80157
970-241-3355
jhadley@FRC.city.com

Dr. Sam Pierpont
Director – Sport Management Program
Academic Advisor
Colorado Mesa University
1100 North Ave.
Grand Junction, CO 81501
970-296-5553
rpierpont@coloradomesa.edu

Resume Checklist

Use the following to evaluate your work:

☐ *Overall format*

No longer than one page (unless extensive experience)

Font is between 10 – 12 point and professional (Times/Garamond)

Pleasing to the eye; balanced white space and use of margins

Effective use of bolding, italics and columns to distinguish key information

Uses bullets to facilitate scanning (no periods)

Well organized into logical sections

Information listed in reverse chronological order and includes dates of participation

Final draft is saved as a PDF to avoid formatting changes

☐ *Content*

There are no spelling or grammatical errors

Verb tenses are consistent

Descriptions begin with action verbs and do not contain "I," "me" or "my"

Contact information is updated and appropriate

References are not included

☐ *Job Specific*

Objective or summary statement is targeted to job, internship or graduate school

Relevant experience and skills are highlighted and appear on the top half of the page

Language is relevant to and shows knowledge of the industry

☐ *Education Section*

Each institution listed includes: name, location, graduate date, degree, major, GPA (optional and only if above 3.0)

Degree is spelled out (Bachelor of Arts…)

Reverse chronological order is used

Distinguished scholarship and honors are listed (may be included in separate section)

Study abroad listed

Relevant research listed (may be included in separate section)

☐ *Experience Section*

Reverse chronological order is used

Information is well defined and includes: organization name, position, location and dates, and duties

Experience is relevant to the intended position; keywords from position are included

Bulleted duty statements begin with strong action verbs

Results are quantified (use numbers when possible)

Skills and accomplishments are clearly illustrated

Internships (may be added as an additional section)

☐ *Skills Section*

Skills listed are relevant to the position

Section is organized and easy to understand

Level of proficiency is indicated for language/computer skills

☐ *Additional Sections* (Honors/Awards, Community Involvement)

Additional sections are appropriate and add to the resume

Activities are listed and description includes skills gained and leadership roles held

Activities are recent, relevant, and include dates

☐ *References*

Reverences are included on a separate document

Three – five professional references are listed

Information is up to date and includes: contact name, position, phone number and email

The Curriculum Vitae

The curriculum vitae or CV is generally used when applying for a teaching or research position in a higher education setting, or perhaps when applying for an exhibition or performance opportunity, which requires a comprehensive list of past related work and experiences. A curriculum vitae, then, is a very specialized type of resume that requires greater depth and breadth of an applicant's professional history, and is usually two or more pages in length. Because this specialized resume includes more than one page, headings on all pages should be the same. Copy and paste your heading with your contact information at the top of each additional page.

Again, many of the rules for the order of information are similar to those for a resume. Reverse chronological order for education background, work history and research or publications. Just like a resume, headings and information used must be selected based on the requirements for the job and the unique background of the applicant. An example follows.

Curriculum Vitae

Bradford Ryckman

Assistant Professor
Interdisciplinary Science Building (ISB) 215
University of Montana, Missoula, MT
406-657-7209

Education

2003-2009   Postdoctoral Training, Oregon Health and Science, Portland, OR

2003   Ph.D. University of Iowa, Iowa City, IA

1997   B.S., Winona State University, Winona, MN

Research Interests

Molecular biology of human cytomegalovirus (HCMV) replication.

Current research goals:

1) To characterize the glycoprotein complexes present in the HCMV envelope that mediate attachment and entry.

2) To define the mechanisms by which HCMV enters different types of cells.

3) To better understand the specific roles of epithelial and endothelial cells in the pathogenesis of HCMV disease.

Employment History

Assistant Professor, Cellular, Molecular, and Microbial Biology, University of Montana, 2009 – Present

Postdoctoral Assistant, Biological Sciences, Oregon Health and Science, Portland, OR, 2003 - 2009

Curriculum Vitae

Bradford Ryckman

Assistant Professor
Interdisciplinary Science Building (ISB) 215
University of Montana, Missoula, MT
406-657-7209

Selected Publications

- 2016
  - Schultz E.P., Lanchy, J.M., Ellerbeck, E.E., Ryckman B.J. Scanning mutagenesis of human cytomegalovirus gH/gL. J.Virol. 90(5):2294-2305
- 2015
  - Zhou M, Lanchy J.M, Ryckman B.J. Human Cytomegalovirus gH/gL/gO Promotes the Fusion Step of Entry into All Cell Types, whereas gH/gL/UL128-131 Broadens Virus Tropism through a Distinct Mechanism. J Virol. 89(17):8999-9009.
  - Li G., Nguyen C.C., Ryckman B.J., Britt W.J., Kamil J.P. A viral regulator of glycoprotein complexes contributes to human cytomegalovirus cell tropism. Proc Natl Acad Sci U S A. 2015 Apr 7;112(14):4471-6
- 2013
  - Zhou M, Yu Q, Wechsler A, Ryckman BJ. (2013) Comparative Analysis of gO Isoforms Reveals that Strains of Human Cytomegalovirus Differ in the Ratio of gH/gL/gO and gH/gL/UL128-131 in the Virion Envelope. J. Virol. 87:9680-9690.
  - Wille PT, Wisner TW, Ryckman B, Johnson DC. Human cytomegalovirus (HCMV) glycoprotein gB promotes virus entry in trans acting as the viral fusion protein rather than as a receptor-binding protein. MBio. 4(3):e00332-13.
- 2010
  - Ryckman,B.J., M.C. Chase, and D.C. Johnson. Human cytomegalovirus TR strain glycoprotein O acts as a chaperone promoting gH/gL incorporation into virions but is not present in virions. J. Virol. 84:2597-2609
- 2008
  - Ryckman,B.J., M.C. Chase, and D.C. Johnson. HCMV gH/gL/UL128-131 interferes with virus entry into epithelial cells: evidence for cell type-specific receptors. Proc. Natl. Acad. Sci. 105:14118-14123.
  - Ryckman, B.J., B. Rainish, M.C. Chase, J. Borton, M.A. Jarvis, J.A. Nelson and D.C. Johnson. Characterization of the HCMV gH/gL/UL128-131 complex that mediates entry into epithelial and endothelial cells. J. Virol. 82:60-70.
- 2006
  - Ryckman, B.J., M.A. Jarvis, D.D. Drummond, J.A. Nelson and D.C. Johnson. Human cytomegalovirus entry into epithelial and endothelial cells depends on genes UL128 to UL150 and occurs by endocytosis and low-pH fusion. J. Virol. 80:710-722.

Using Social Media

Facebook

Companies frequently have Facebook accounts set up to showcase work projects, highlight employees and share their involvement in the local community. Employers also use Facebook as a screening tool, checking out applicants before narrowing down their list of candidates and deciding who to interview. If your Facebook page contains images and links that you would not want a potential employer to view, you may want to do some clean-up work before sending out your resume.

LinkedIn

LinkedIn is the professional version of Facebook, and it would be to your advantage to have a presence there. Creating an account is free. You can upload your resume, add a professional looking photograph, and highlight major accomplishments and skills that you would like a potential employer to see. You can also import media if you have a portfolio to share. You will want to include your LinkedIn URL as part of your contact information at the top of your resume. A brief overview of setting up a LinkedIn page follows.

Creating a LinkedIn Profile

Tips before you begin:

Create your resume first and use it as a resource to copy and paste your information to LinkedIn.

1. Go to www.linkedin.com and join.
2. Use a personal e-mail that looks professional and a password that you can remember.
3. You will have an option to notify your e-mail contacts to connect with you if they are on LinkedIn. You may choose to skip this step.
4. You will have an option to add APPs for mobile devices.
5. When you visit your account, a blue box will appear asking questions that will help build your profile. Some revolve around work experience and your duties. Be specific.
6. Create a **HEADLINE** for yourself. Tell what your job/major is.
7. Upload a **PHOTO** that looks professional. A nice top/shirt and your best smile will do.
8. You will have to click on "Edit Profile" to add items or make changes.
9. Add a **SUMMARY** and describe what you'd like known about yourself in a nutshell.
10. List the jobs you've held with what you accomplished in each, in the **EXPERIENCE** section (use your resume).
11. Add your current degree information in the **EDUCATION** section.
12. You can add **ADDITIONAL INFORMATION** by clicking on "edit" under the Background section and choosing any of the headings to the right of your profile. You might include projects, languages, publications, organizations, honors & awards, courses, certifications and volunteering.

Creating a professional profile is just the beginning. Literally thousands of companies have a presence on LinkedIn. Many of their employees also have accounts. You can learn a lot about a company and its leaders by visiting their LinkedIn account.

Take advantage of the groups that are available on LinkedIn. Groups are initiated by professionals in a particular field. For example, a search for "geologist groups" yielded 121 results. You will need to apply to become part of a group, but this is usually just a formality. Through these organizations, you can follow current discussion in the industry, learn about job openings and network with professionals in the field.

The Big Idea

*The key word here is **professional**. Once you begin that professional job search, everything a potential employer sees must look and sound professional. From your resume and cover letter, to the photo on your LinkedIn account and the information on your Facebook page. It must all convey, "I am a professional and am worthy of a professional job."*

Write a Cover Letter

A resume is mandatory. For many jobs, a cover letter is optional. The thing a cover letter can do for you, however, is bring particular coursework, an internship, related job experience, or a personal strength to life. Sometimes a cover letter may set you apart from someone who chooses not to include one, and it allows a potential employer to get to know you a little better.

If you choose to write a cover letter, it must:

- Be well-written and error-free
- Be organized
- Specifically illustrate your qualifications for a position

A cover letter should be written in a business letter format. Block style is easiest because you don't ever have to indent! You'll want to include your address, the date, the address of the employer, and a greeting. If you're not sure what a block style letter looks like, do an Internet search and find a copy.

Sometimes letters are hard to write. The tendency is to write everything you can think of and put it all in one huge paragraph. Here are some guidelines that may help you organize your information. Begin by researching the company's website and learn all that you can.

Paragraph 1: Explain why you are writing this letter. You can share how you learned about their opening and why you would like to work for their organization.

For example, *"Please accept my application for the position of Designer with ABC Branding. I learned of the position through my college career center, and would be excited to work for a company that contributes to organizations for the homeless throughout the country."*

Paragraph 2: Highlight your education and work experience that is relevant to the job for which you are applying.

"As you can see from my resume, I recently completed my degree in graphic design, graduating with honors. One of the highlights of my college program was the opportunity to participate in an internship with Denver Advertising, where I performed as a member of the design team. One of the most important things I learned was to research information on competitors before attempting a new advertising design for a client. A quality advertising design must be a unique, fresh idea, and it can't be similar to one another company uses. It was my job to perform this research on four different industries and bring the information to the design team to provide adequate background information. With this critical information in hand, our design team was better equipped to provide quality design recommendations for clients."

Paragraph 3: State personal qualities or strengths and how they relate to the job.

"In addition to my education and work experience, I have several strengths that will enable me to be a great addition to your creative team at ABC Branding. I am a very focused and goal-oriented individual in addition to being an effective team member. Once I have established my job target, I create a detailed plan and timeline that drives my work. During my internship at Denver Advertising, I contributed as a team member to plan a strategy for the needs of a particular client. As a group, we established a timeline for the work that led to the finished project and presentation of that work to the client. Those are strengths and strategies I would bring to your organization."

Paragraph 4: Restate your interest in the position. Thank them for their consideration.

"I am very interested in this position and believe it would be a good match for my skills and education. I look forward to visiting with you about the job, and would be happy to come for an interview at your convenience. Please feel free to contact me by email (*asmith@gmail.com*) or by phone (303-982-4432). Thank you for your consideration."

Close your letter formally as used in the block style business letter. An example follows.

3055 Smith Road
Littleton, CO 80126

April 2, 2016

Landon Bennett, Manager
Denver Sports
1575 California Street
Denver, CO 80202

Dear Mr. Bennett:

Please accept my application for the position of Sports Manager with Denver Sports. I learned of the job through my advisor at the Department of Kinesiology at Colorado Mesa University. I am very interested in working for an organization that is at the forefront in promoting a variety of sports and a healthy lifestyle to the Denver area.

As you can see from my resume, I earned a Bachelor of Science degree in Sport Management from Colorado Mesa University, while participating on the CMU soccer team. Specialized coursework as well as authentic opportunities to apply my learning, have prepared me well for this position. I especially benefitted from working with the management team at the Grand Junction Rockies during my academic internship.

In addition to my education, I have many skills that will enable me to be an asset to your management team at Denver Sports. I bring management experience from a variety of settings, including a summer position where I served as manager/coach for Soccer Camps Incorporated in Boulder. I did the recruiting, training, scheduling, and managed the budget for a traveling team of 12 to 14 year-old players. My internship experience with the Grand Junction Rockies also allowed me to utilize my management, as well as marketing and supervisory skills, in a sports setting. I believe my eight-year career as a soccer athlete, nurtured my understanding of and passion for team sports. This is an enthusiasm I am excited to share with others.

I am very interested in this position and believe my education and background make me a good match for the job requirements. I would be happy to come for an interview at your convenience. Please feel free to contact me by phone (303-335-5424), or email (sparkm@gmail.com). Thank you for your consideration, and I look forward to hearing from you.

Sincerely yours,

Steven Parkman

THE BIG IDEA!

This is where you sell yourself. Highlight those experiences from your education and work, as well as personal strengths that make you the best candidate for the job. This is your opportunity to bring something to life from your resume. Use your own voice and an effective writing style. It is also an opportunity to show a potential employer your skills in written communication. Make sure your letter is free of errors.

Delivering Your Information

Your finished product will depend on how your resume and cover letter need to be delivered for a particular job. You may have the opportunity to hand-deliver or snail-mail your information to an employer. That means you have control over the print quality and appearance of your credentials.

MAILING OR HAND-DELIVERING YOUR INFORMATION

Print your resume, cover letter, and reference page on resume-quality paper. No crazy colors or designs. Choose either a white or off-white paper.

Invest in a 9 x 12 clasp-type manila envelope to contain your application materials. Clearly print the name, title, and address of the person to whom you are sending your materials in the center of the envelope. Include your return address in the top, left-hand corner. Include sufficient postage for mailing your materials.

Use a paper clip (do not staple!) to attach your materials in this order: cover letter on top, resume, reference page, completed application form (if required), and transcripts (if needed).

UPLOADING YOUR MATERIALS ELECTRONICALLY

Make sure all files fit correctly on the page. If you have a resume that is more than one page, make sure you have pasted your heading at the top of the second page. Never begin an additional page with information left dangling from the previous page. Always begin with a complete section, including the heading, when beginning another page.

Save all files to be sent in a PDF format. You don't want to chance any tampering with your information, or that once downloaded, the formatting makes your information confusing to read. Save your files under an easily recognizable file name that includes your name: StevenParkmanResume. pdf. That way an employer can easily keep your materials together.

FOLLOW ALL SUBMISSION DIRECTIONS

Employers often have very different instructions for sending your information. Make sure you follow their directions exactly. If you are to simply upload your files by browsing for them on the computer, then sending them, do that. Some instructions may specify to e-mail your files by attaching them, using a particular title in in the subject line, or including your cover letter in the body of your e-mail instead of an attachment. Whatever the directions, read them carefully, and follow them.

STORE A PLAIN-TEXT COPY OF YOUR WORK

Keep a plain-text copy of your work on your computer. If you're submitting your resume via a web-based submission system rather than e-mailing it, you'll often need to copy and paste different sections of the document into different parts of the employer's web form, including online applications. Having a plain-text, unformatted resume on hand for these opportunities can make this process a lot easier. Just "save as" and choose "plain text" when saving another version of your work.

ALWAYS INCLUDE A COVER LETTER

Even if directions do not mention a cover letter, always include one with your resume. This sets you apart from those who choose not to include one, and allows you to bring some important things to life from your resume. Do not include other materials, such as transcripts or references unless they are specifically asked for, however. Save these materials and bring them to the interview in case you have an opportunity to refer to them.

Job Searching Strategies

Searching for a job requires some creativity, definitely professionalism and certainly, persever-ance. Unless you are one of those lucky individuals who steps right from an internship to a pro-fessional job, you have to be prepared to develop a job-searching plan and stick to it until you land that dream career.

UTILIZE YOUR COLLEGE CAREER CENTER
Go to the professionals who have the expertise and are on your very own campus. College career folks have specialized training and experience in evaluating your resume and cover letter and focus-ing on jobs for which you are qualified and how to locate them. They often offer workshops on job searching and host career fairs. Career centers also have online job boards, of which you need to be a regular user. You can make an appointment at your convenience, but it is better to do it sooner than later.

NETWORK
Studies show that between fifty and eighty percent of all jobs are never advertised. Hiring managers often rely on recommendations from colleagues instead of traditional recruiting because they know the qualifications immediately and that the individual comes recommended. For this reason, you must let as many people know that you are looking for a job and what kind. Begin with individuals who work in your particular field and network with them—family friends and neighbors, community members, faculty and staff and fellow students at your school. Take advantage of your LinkedIn ac-count and search for companies for which you would like to work. Search for employees who have the job you would like, connect with them, and ask what they enjoy about their position and the company. You might even inquire what would be the best way to approach the company about a

job. Join LinkedIn groups in your field. Follow the discussion to "listen in" to what is going on in the industry. Ask questions and participate in the discussion. This is a great opportunity to network with professionals who will notice you and answer questions you have. In addition, attend conferences and professional meetings and introduce yourself. Often, it is who you know that gets you the job—or at least an interview.

CREATE A LINKEDIN PROFILE
LinkedIn is a great source of professional jobs. First, however, update your profile. Scrutinize other profiles and find out what makes them stand out. Upload a copy of your dynamite resume and a professional looking photo. Create a unique, but professional headline. Include internships and related work experience and a list of your professional skills and strengths. Attach links to your portfolio of professional work including research, published work, presentations and other appropriate material. List groups and organizations of which you are a member. Once you have your profile ready to be looked at by an employer, search under the jobs tab for jobs in your field by location.

TARGET EMPLOYERS DIRECTLY
Many large employers only advertise on their own website. Locate company websites and apply for jobs there. You may find that these companies do not have job openings listed on their site. If this is a company for which you would really like to work, put together your resume and a letter of inquiry and email them to the human resources director. Visit the company, if it is local, and take a copy of your resume and letter to the office. Try to arrange an informational interview, which might include a tour of the facility and the opportunity to ask questions about the organization, jobs available, and how you might fit into the picture.

ATTEND CAREER FAIRS
Career fairs are hosted by college career centers and departments, county and state workforce centers, Individual companies, and various organizations. Dress up, take several copies of your resume and network. It is helpful to prepare a brief statement about yourself and your qualifications, sometimes referred to as an elevator pitch, to confidently share your educational background, skills and experience with a potential employer.

USE YOUR LOCAL COMMUNITY JOB CENTER
Each state has a branch of its state job system located in each county and often in other locations within the county. Individuals can create an online account and have jobs postings emailed to them as they become available. Local job centers also host hiring events for employers in the area or new businesses just beginning. Many also offer assistance with job searching by appointment.

APPLY TO CLASSIFIED ADS IN THE NEWSPAPER

Employers still advertise through newspapers, but you'll want to use the online version to search for jobs. Often the Sunday edition of a paper offers the best listing of jobs available.

USE PROFESSIONAL ASSOCIATIONS

Every career area has one or more professional organizations. You may have belonged to the student affiliated organization when you were in college. Just do an Internet search to find the organizations for your profession ("Professional associations for geologists"). These organizations have informative websites and usually job boards. Because professionals pay membership fees to participate in these organizations, sought-after employers often post jobs on the site's job board. Professional organizations hold regional and annual conferences, as well, which are excellent opportunities to network and learn about jobs.

SEARCH ELECTRONIC JOB SITES

The number of electronic recruiting sites seems to grow daily! Find the best ones that provide the most return for your time and visit those on a regular basis. Your college career center will have recommendations for you and may have a list of recommended sites on their web page. Remember to include your college career center job board on your search list. The key to successful electronic searches is to be creative with your search terms. Create a list of the specific job titles for which you want to search. For example, if your degree is in environmental science, you could search for "environmental scientist, field scientist, geoscientist, environmental engineer, and environmentalist." A good site to visit for federal jobs is *usajobs.gov*.

USE TEMPORARY EMPLOYMENT AGENCIES

When you're looking for that professional job, you have to pursue every avenue. You may need employment to pay the bills while searching for that permanent professional position. Temporary agencies are looking for individuals with a wide variety of skills. Often, they need someone to step right in a professional job because of an emergency situation, and sometimes this leads to full-time employment. If you are available and do a good job, supervisors get to know you and your work ethic. And if the regular employee is unable to return to the job, it may be yours. So don't discount temporary agencies because of the stereotype they may have.

VOLUNTEER INTO A CAREER

Individuals can gain valuable skills by volunteering with a company or organization. Look for an organization where you might begin working on skills you would use in your field of study. Nonprofit organizations are often shorthanded and welcome volunteers. Many large organizations, like health care facilities, often employ a volunteer coordinator. In any event, you can present your resume to someone in the human resources department and offer your services. Serving as a volunteer is also a terrific opportunity to network with professionals that may be helpful in assisting you in locating openings in your career area. If you are lucky, a job opening may occur while you are assisting in a volunteer capacity, and you may be considered. In addition, community service looks great on your resume.

THE BIG IDEA!

Searching for a professional job is almost a full-time job. You need to search a variety of places and document with whom you have applied, contact information and dates. Treat each application process as an opportunity for networking. The more professionals you meet, the better your chances of being considered for that professional position.

You Got The Interview!

The hiring committee liked your resume, so they read on. They liked what you highlighted in your cover letter and they decided they need to meet you.

Remember, the interview process is a two-way street. You are interviewing the company as much as the interview committee is learning about you. They learn about you and your qualifications for the job, and you learn about their organization and its people.

Being prepared pays off! A big part of your interview success depends on the work you do *before* it takes place.

BEFORE THE INTERVIEW

RESEARCH THE COMPANY
Look at their website and find out:

- What they do
- Where they do business – are they a global organization?
- Mission and vision statements
- Staff development offerings/benefits
- Community involvement

Look at their *LinkedIn* and *Facebook* accounts.
Learn as much about the company as you can.

KNOW THE JOB DESCRIPTION
You already familiarized yourself with it to create your resume and cover letter. Make sure you know it backwards and forwards in case you get asked about any of the duties in your interview and your

qualifications for performing them. Be ready to talk about how your skills and education make you a good match for the requirements of the job.

CHOOSE YOUR WARDROBE

First impressions are important. Dress conservatively, and dress up. Dressing up makes you feel professional as well as look professional.

- *Tips for men:*
  Grey, black, or navy dress pants and jacket
  White or light blue shirt
  Tie with simple stripes or small pattern
  Black belt and lace-up shoes and socks
- *Tips for women:*
  Gray, black, or navy skirt and jacket or pantsuit
  White or pastel blouse
  Black shoes, belt and bag
  Simple, quiet jewelry

Make sure your outfit is comfortable when you are sitting, standing or walking, and that your clothing is clean and pressed. You can almost pretend you are dressing for a date. Everything should be clean and simple. Hair, nails, teeth, and make-up.

Avoid things that can distract from your interview: Piercings, trendy or revealing clothing, tattoos, facial hair, overpowering perfumes.

PRACTICE YOUR GREETING

No, handshakes are not out of date. They are a strong, appropriate tool that shows you can handle yourself in professional situations. Practice on your family. Practice on your friends. Smile, offer your hand, and provide a strong handshake. Introduce yourself and tell your interviewer that you are very happy to meet him/her. It is appropriate, if a small interview team (2-5 individuals) to shake everyone's hand before you are seated. If it is a larger group, just smile at the group, introduce yourself and let them know you are happy to meet them and be present for the interview.

PRACTICE INTERVIEW QUESTIONS

Just like any other activity at which you want to improve, you practice. That's how you get better at the piano, golf, or art. The more you practice, the more you improve, and the *more confidence you have. There are some questions that are common to almost any interview. Practice out loud. It is important that your brain hears your voice answering the questions. It is ok to write answers to the questions, but then go over them orally several times without looking at your notes. Here is another valuable service of your college career center. Career professionals often provide mock interviews. They create a professional environment where you participate in a very authentic interview experience. Take advantage of their expertise.*

What are the most common interview questions?
Can you tell me a little about yourself?
Why did you decide to become a _____?
What do you know about our company?
Why do you want this particular position?
What are 3 strengths that you would bring to this job?
Where do you see yourself in five years?
What is one weakness that you have?
What do you feel is an important issue in your field today?
Give an example of when you had a conflict with a coworker.
Why should we hire you?
What questions do you have for the interview team?

These are the questions most common to every interview.

Now, how should you answer these?
Can you tell me a little about yourself?

This question is not giving you the opportunity to delve into all of your childhood experiences. When an interviewer asks this question, what they want to know is, "Tell me about yourself as it relates to this position." You may start out by mentioning where you are from, but quickly jump to what sparked your interest in this career, your college preparation, and any internship, related job or volunteer experience that confirmed that this is the right match for you. End by stating your interest in this position because it will provide an opportunity to practice all that you've learned and contribute to the company. Tell them you are appreciative of the opportunity to interview with them.

Why did you decide to become a _____?

You fill in the blank. Whatever the career title is, do not respond with general statements. "I love kids. I like to work with my hands." These are the lines everyone comes up with. Tell what sparked your interest in your field. Be specific. Use detail. And most important, let your enthusiasm for your chosen career show in your voice and body language. And follow up with volunteer, shadowing or work experience that confirmed your choice. Talk briefly about coursework, internships, clubs or conferences that continued to foster your interest and commitment to your major. End by noting how this job will enable you to put all of those skills and experiences into practice and that you are extremely excited for that opportunity.

What do you know about our company? Why do you want to work for us?

If you have trouble answering this one, you're in big trouble. Here is where your homework pays off. Visit the company website thoroughly. Know exactly what they do and where. What goals do they have (mission and vision statements)? Have they won an award? Do they have outstanding sales for the past year? Are they trying innovative ideas? Do they provide great staff development? Are employees offered opportunities to be involved in the community? Find out enough information so you can answer these questions thoroughly and without hesitation.

Why do you want this particular position?

Don't let it be the case of you need a job and they have one. Describe how this position offers you the opportunity to put into practice what you have learned in your coursework and your internship. Cite specifically what parts of the job about which you are particularly interested and how well your education has prepared you. Again, be specific if possible. You can include personal strengths that lend themselves to this position. End by sharing your excitement about this particular opportunity with their organization and being able to learn and work with their outstanding professionals.

What are three strengths that you would bring to this job?

What are your strong points? Choose things that would definitely be an asset in this position, and if they are in the job description qualification list, that would be a plus. Have three strengths well in mind, with a brief illustration of how you have used each effectively. There should be no hesitation with this question. For example, you may consider your skill in collaboration a major strength. Then briefly discuss your involvement on an internship team that successfully created a website that brought business growth to the company for which it was designed. Again, specifics are important. Will you be asked for 3? Who knows? But if you're ready with this answer, your confidence will shine.

Where do you see yourself in five years?

Interviewers ask this question because they want to know if you are goal-oriented and if you'll be using their position as a stepping stone to bigger and better things. You can answer this in general terms using your field of study. Explain that in five years you hope to be in a position where you can continue to make a positive difference in customer service, student learning, or company growth. You hope to learn and grow as a professional so you can make a strong contribution in your field, and are looking forward to that role with this particular company. Although this question does not limit your answer to professional information, you want to keep your thoughts geared toward your professional career rather than your personal goals.

What is one weakness that you have?

Everyone has something at which they are not so good. A potential employer just wants to know you recognize that you have an area that needs help and that you are addressing it. For example, often students tend to take on too much because they find it difficult to say *no*. As this is recognized to be a problem, the next time someone asks you to do something you know won't fit into your schedule, simply tell them you'd like to help them but you know your schedule is busy. You may tell them you'll think about it and get back to them. At least that gives you some think time, and time to look at your schedule. You can let them know that you won't be able to help this time, but to ask you again at another time. Never choose a weakness that is going to throw an obstacle in your way of getting a job.

What do you feel is an important issue in your field today?

Hopefully, discussions that you've had in your classes will help you with this one. Certainly, have a couple of topics that have become important issues in your area of study that could be discussed. Again, here is where a little research is helpful when you go to your interview.

Give an example of when you had a conflict with a coworker.

You can count on a question like this in every interview. A potential employer wants to know how you handle yourself when things don't go as planned. Every job has some conflict, so be ready with an answer that shows you in a positive light. You don't have to go into a lot of detail. Briefly describe the situation, what you did, and what the results were. If you don't have a work situation, you might talk about a classroom group or an organization or team conflict that you experienced. It doesn't have to be a major conflict. A situation where a misunderstanding occurred will work. Choose an experience that had a positive outcome if possible. You want to illustrate your problem-solving and interpersonal skills with your experience.

Why should we hire you?

This should be a question on which you don't hesitate. There are lots of qualified candidates. Why should they hire you for this position? If you have your three strengths well in mind from the earlier question, you can streamline that answer for this question and deliver it with a big smile and all the enthusiasm you can muster. Know your strengths and what you would bring to this job. Convince your interviewers that you are the one.

What questions do you have for the interview team?

Once the interview team is finished with their formal questions, they will generally offer you the opportunity to ask any questions you might have. You will always need to have 4-5 questions prepared to ask the interview team. Some of your questions may already have been answered during your interview, so go with the remaining ones on your list. Choose meaningful questions. Information that can easily be found on the company's website should not be included; however you may want the group to elaborate on something you read on their site. You may have read that the company offers opportunities for employees to be involved as volunteers in the community, and can ask for more information. Based on the position up for grabs, you might ask the team to describe their ideal candidate. This is also a nice opportunity to allow the interviewers to talk about their positions and the success of their efforts and their company. "Share a company (or department) achievement that you are excited about." "What is something you are really looking forward to this coming year?"

Be prepared for nonsense questions.

If you could be an animal, what would you be? You may think this is a nonsense question, but the interview team is trying to learn more about you as a person. Maybe they want to see if you have a sense of humor or how you react to an unpredictable situation. Relax, and have fun with this question. Let your creativity show through.

Some questions not to bring up.

Don't ask about salary during your interview. Have a job offer in place, then you can negotiate. Be prepared to discuss this when THEY bring it up, usually at the time of a job offer. Internship salary or hourly rate is usually predetermined by the company and rarely negotiable. Know what the salary range is for the type of work environment and location. Research www.salary.com, www.rileyguide.com, www.wetfeet.com, and www.bls.gov.

Discriminatory Questions

Questions can only center on your qualifications and ability to do the job. Asking for information that isn't essential to evaluating a person's qualifications leaves the employer vulnerable to charges of discrimination. Be careful in casual discussions about sharing unnecessary information. Laws vary from state to state.

Examples:

Age
Marital of family status and pregnancy
Race, ethnicity, or color

Religion
Disability
Gender or sex
Country of national origin

What if you're asked a discriminatory question?

For example: Is child care going to be an issue for you?

You have three choices:

- You are free to answer but must understand you are providing personal information that is not job-related.
- You can refuse to answer, but might run the risk of appearing uncooperative or confrontational.
- You can think about the intent behind the question and answer accordingly. Do they simply want reassurance that you will be dependable and prompt in your work habits? An appropriate, job-related answer might be: "I can meet the work schedule that the job requires."

BE READY FOR DIFFERENT KINDS OF INTERVIEWS

Phone Interviews

Dress up. You will feel more confident when answering questions.

Use a dependable phone. *Choose a connection you know will maintain strong reception and be distraction free.*

Give yourself time*. Allow enough time to adequately answer the questions. No lunch break interviews.*

Be ready. *Have a copy of your resume, the job description and Internet access to the company website.*

Answer confidently with your name.

Smile and let your enthusiasm show through in your voice.

Convince your interviewers that you are the person for the job.

Individual, Face-to-Face Interviews

This is the most common interview setting. You are interviewed by two or more company employees. Generally the setting is a conference area at the company's location.

Dress professionally.

Shake hands and introduce yourself to all interviewers.

Seat yourself comfortably, but professionally. Let your hands rest in your lap.

Body language says it all. Be relaxed, but be alert. Let your expression, voice and body radiate enthusiasm.

Lunch or Dinner Interviews

Dress professionally. You will feel more confident and look like a professional.

Use your manners. Sign up for an etiquette dinner to learn and practice proper dining protocol.

Order food that is easy to eat (no spaghetti) and not the most expensive on the menu.

Be yourself, but appropriate. One purpose behind a dinner interview is for company personnel to get to know you.

Online Interviews

Dress professionally. Even if you are sitting down, wear nice pants and shoes (you never know when you might have to stand up).

Clear your workspace and any clutter that is behind you so it doesn't show up on the monitor.

Make sure you are in a quiet room where you will not be disturbed by people, pets, etc.

Have a notepad and pen in case you need to write down something important.

Have a copy of your resume in sight, in case you have to refer to something.

Practice. Practice using your webcam equipment before the interview so you are sure everything is in working order.

Group Interviews

- Group interviews involve bringing you into an interview with several other candidates who are vying for the same position. All candidates in the group are interviewed simultaneously.
- The interviewers in these situations are interested in how you respond and react to other candidates, as well as how you respond to questions directed at you.

Behave in a polite manner toward other candidates.

Be alert and ready to interact.

Don't be shy— be interactive. Praise good responses of others, using those as a transition to your own.

Include quieter candidates. This shows teamwork.

Speak with purpose. Your preparation builds confidence.

Be yourself, but as a part of the interview group.

Be prepared to complete a performance portion of the interview.

Depending on the job for which you are applying, you may be asked to perform in one of the roles expected as part of the job. Usually you are informed of this before you come for the interview, but not always.

Examples include:

Creating office documents such as a spreadsheet, business letter or memo
Giving a presentation
Conducting a meeting
Teaching a lesson
Addressing an athletic injury
Participating in a panel discussion
Creating a plan for something

INTERVIEW DAY

Your interview begins the moment you step from your car!

Arrive a little early – 15 minutes or so—so you know where you need to be.
Be on time!
Leave your cell phone in your car.
Bring a notepad with your questions for the interview team and a pen.
Bring an extra copy of your resume.
Bring a copy of your portfolio.
Greet everyone with a smile and handshake.
Look at the interviewer as you answer questions.
Be friendly and enthusiastic!
Think about each question thoughtfully, and answer in a calm, organized manner.
At the end of the interview, ask the questions you have practiced, unless they have already been addressed during the interview.
Thank the interviewer(s) for their time.
Tell them you are very interested in the job, and you look forward to hearing from them.

AFTER THE INTERVIEW, FOLLOW UP

Send a written note to the chairperson of the interview team, thanking him/her for the opportunity to interview with their company. Express your interest in the position, and tell them you look forward to hearing from them.

Have they made a decision? Wait a full week after your interview, then call the personnel manager to see if a decision has been made. If the group is still in the decision-making process, ask about the timeline for a decision.

Be positive and wait for the call. If you land the job, way to go! If you don't get the job, make sure not to close any doors. It is appropriate to touch base with the company periodically and remind them of your interest in their organization. Keep these individuals in your network.

Most importantly, stay positive. Look at each interview as an opportunity to gain practice and confidence. Stick to your plan. Organize your work.

Troubleshooting for Job Seekers

The Problem: You are unable to find adequate jobs for which you are qualified.
Suggestion: Search for different types of jobs that are attainable with your degree and qualifications. Work with a professional to brainstorm possible job titles. You may need to expand your list of terms you are using in which to search for positions. Try some different job search websites. Again, a professional can help you make a list of sites to search.

The Problem: You are sending out resumes, but are receiving no calls from employers.
Suggestion: Your resume is not attracting interest. Make sure you are customizing your resume specifically for the requirements of the jobs for which you are applying. Your resume may include good information, but it may not show any relevance to potential employers. Work with a career professional to create a resume that is tailored for each position sought. Does your resume have a professional look that is free of errors? Have others evaluate your resume before you send it off.

The Problem: You are being invited to interview, but never get the job.
Suggestion: The more you practice, the more confident you become in answering questions effectively. Make sure you are well versed in the company with whom you are interviewing. Know the information on their website thoroughly. Be very familiar with the job description and requirements, and be able to demonstrate your qualifications for it. Schedule a mock interview session with a career professional to polish your skills.

THE BIG IDEA!

Your job search needs to be continual and constant. Continue your plan of sending out applications on a regular basis, touch base with employers previously contacted, and keep your skills sharp. Stay organized and persistent. If you're not successful in obtaining an interview, or a position after an interview, schedule an appointment with a career services professional to have your resume evaluated, do some job searching, and practice your interviewing skills.

Diana Barnett works as a career counselor at Colorado Mesa University, helping college students prepare to enter the professional world. She has taught all of her students that the key to the perfect career is finding the one that aligns with each individual's strengths, personality, passion, and abilities.

Barnett holds a bachelor of arts degree and a master's degree in education from the University of Montana and has written two other books, *Putting It All Together: Teaching the Research Process* and *Research It! Write It!*

She currently lives near Grand Junction, Colorado, in the country with her husband, dog, and two cats.

Additional resources can be found on the author's website at redrockscareercoaching.wordpress.com.

59377084R00033

Made in the USA
Charleston, SC
02 August 2016